Old Shetland Country Life

David Pettigrew

Oxen-drawn carts on Fair Isle, which lies 27 miles north of Orkney and 24 miles south of Shetland, to which it officially belongs. These distances make it the most remote inhabited island in the UK. People have lived on Fair Isle since Neolithic times. Farming and fishing have always been mainstays of the island's economy, sustaining a population of around four hundred in 1900. Numbers were already dropping by this time as many had emigrated to North America. The population in 2021 was 48. Visiting in 1869, Robert Louis Stevenson described the place as 'an unhomely, rugged turret-top of submarine sierras' though he was also inspired to compose the lovely short poem 'Fair Isle at sea': *Fair Isle at sea – thy lovely name / Soft in my ear like music came / That sea I loved, and once or twice / I touched at isles of Paradise.*

Text © David Pettigrew, 2024.
First published in the United Kingdom, 2024,
by Stenlake Publishing Ltd.,
54-58 Mill Square,
Catrine, Ayrshire,
KA5 6RD

Telephone: 01290 551122
www.stenlake.co.uk

ISBN 9781840339840

Printed by:
P2D,
1 Newlands Road,
Westoning, MK45 5LD

The publishers regret that they cannot supply copies of any pictures featured in this book.

A number of books, articles and websites were consulted for the research of this book. A list of these is obtainable from the publisher on request.

Fair Isle is very well known for Fair Isle sweaters, knitwear characterised by geometric patterns which have been exported from the islands since the 1860s though only gained widespread popularity from the 1920s after Edward, Prince of Wales, wore one as part of his golfing attire. The origins of the patterns are not known – possibly they came from Norse settlers or Spanish sailors of the Armada of 1588 who had been blown off-course – but the women of the Isle were using them in pullovers knitted for the fishermen from the eighteenth century and they were commonly worn by islanders since that time, though none of these Fair Isle fishermen appear to have been given one! The 'Fair Isle' style remains extremely popular though the term has become loosely applied to any clothing carrying a design of this kind. Knitwear is still produced on the island and, much sought after, carries a trademark to guarantee its authenticity.

Introduction

There has been human habitation in Shetland for around 6,000 years and from the very beginning people were farmers rather than hunters. At that time the islands had far more trees than they do now, the climate was warmer and farming was easier. The Picts, also a farming people, settled around 400 AD and their culture lasted for several hundred years until Norse settlers arrived around 800 AD. They too lived off the land, establishing townships that could contain up to twenty houses, each household sharing arable land equally. These areas tended to be enclosed within dykes, leaving livestock to graze on common ground – or 'scathold' – which was usually higher ground beyond.

Shetland became a Scottish possession in 1469 and the age of common ownership of the land was now replaced by feudalism, whereby the people became tenants of lairds, keen to extract as much profit as they could from the people, the land and the waters around it. By this time Shetlanders were using boats brought ready-made from Norway for fishing and they traded cured fish, fish oil, cloth and butter with German merchants who brought rye meal, coinage, fishing gear and household items. Traders from England and Scotland followed their lead and the Dutch became major importers of Shetland fish in the 1600s.

While all these developments were taking place, many Shetlanders remained dependent on crofting which provided subsistence crops of corn, kale and bere (a type of barley that is not commonly grown now). The seventeenth century saw severe famines and smallpox epidemics which kept the population beneath 20,000. Cabbages were introduced as a crop by Cromwellian soldiers stationed at Lerwick and Scalloway and potatoes were introduced around 1730, becoming a dietary staple. Hay and straw was made from the grasslands, but not enough could be produced for winter when many cattle would die of starvation; it was only after turnips were introduced in 1807 that this situation was alleviated.

In 1712 a tariff was imposed on foreign salt and a bounty was given on all fish cured with British salt by British merchants. It allowed the lairds to take this business away from the Dutch and they made it a condition of tenure that crofters had to supply fish such as cod and ling so that they could sell them to German and Spanish markets. This meant the men now had to spend their summers engaged in 'far haaf' fishing in order to pay their rent; this was very dangerous, involving expeditions in open boats that could last for 36 hours. Some crofts were also subdivided to make them too small to provide subsistence crops, forcing the crofters to buy meal from the landlords. In the late 1700s the destitution was such that people started to emigrate, though lairds tried to encourage them to stay by giving them free meal and longer credit on the truck system of goods supply that people were compelled to use. By this time, Greenland whalers were stopping at the islands to recruit crews and 3,200 Shetlanders were in the Royal Navy, often press-ganged, during the Napoleonic wars.

Further depopulation occurred from the 1840s when lairds started to evict crofters in order to create more grazing for sheep, which were now proving more profitable than fish. By 1871 the population was 18,525 females and 13,080 males spread across 28 islands, some of which – including Mousa, Samphray, Bigga, Balta, Papa Little and Vemintry – had been emptied of people and given over to grazing. Over the next ten years emigration increased, with 4,460 people leaving for a new life overseas.

The latter part of the nineteenth century saw changes that improved the lot of many people. In farming, drainage of land became widespread, helping to improve crops. Rye grass, clover and white oats were introduced, yielding greater quantities of grain and straw. The Crofters Holdings Act of 1886 stopped lairds from evicting tenants and the Truck Commission of 1872 ended tenants' obligation to barter their produce on unfavourable terms with lairds and merchants, though the system did continue in some form. In fishing, decked boats were introduced in 1876 and soon steam trawlers were engaged in the growing herring trade largely based on the western side of the islands. Women now took work as herring gutters and packers and men found work on the boats or employment on the whaling ships. Between the 1890s and 1914 there were also around 3,000 Shetlanders in the Merchant Navy.

The twentieth century saw the fishing industry become ever more industrialised and the oil boom of the late 1970s changed the economy of Shetland for ever. Crofting is no longer carried on to the extent it was in previous centuries, though some Shetlanders still work their land while maintaining jobs in the newer industries, keeping the old ways going.

Above: Trondra is one of the Scalloway Islands, a subgroup of the Shetland isles, and lies just south of Scalloway. This image from 1897 shows women carrying creels, while their children look delighted to be having their picture taken on the boat. Boats like this were essential means of transport for people, goods and livestock around and between islands and were also used for fishing. The design of traditional Shetland boats owe much to their Viking predecessors, indeed due to the lack of wood on the islands, from the eighteenth century boats were generally built from kits sent over from Norway (though some were built from driftwood). Generally, there were two standard sizes, one for four oars (a 'fourareen' or 'fourern', derived from the Nordic *færings*, and likely the type in the picture) and one for six oars (a 'sixareen' or 'sixern' derived from *seksærings*). Sails could be used on either. Other Shetland boat types include the Fair Isle yole, the Ness yole, the haddock boat (large and sturdy, used for winter haddock fishing), the eela boat and the maid class sail boat.

Fishing implements dating from 3000 BC have been found on Shetland. 'Haaf' fishing was done within sight of land, while fishing the 'far haaf' could involve going up to 60 miles out to sea. From the late 1700s the sixareen was used for this. Expeditions in these open boats took several days, the men completely exposed to the elements while they fished with lines of up to 6 or 7 miles in length. Many lost their lives in this occupation. The photo shows a crew drying their catch, probably cod. It was taken in the early 1900s and the men would have been able to keep their modest catch to sell or consume themselves. Before the passing of the Crofters Holdings Act of 1886, which guaranteed tenants' rights, fishermen had to give most of their catches up to the laird, or owner of the land on which they lived, to pay their rent. They also rented their boats and gear from the lairds. From the late 1800s, larger boats such as Fifies and Zulus began to be used, as well as steam trawlers, and fishing became increasingly industrialised. With a turnover of tens of millions of pounds, it remains a major part of the Shetland economy today.

Whales were hunted around Shetland for hundreds of years. 'Drive' fishing was the method used to capture Pilot whales – known locally as 'Caain' whales – which congregated in large groups, making it easy to drive large numbers of them into bays. Whole communities would get involved: boats formed a ring around the whales, forcing them inland so they could be dragged ashore and killed with rocks and farm implements, the water literally turning red with whale blood. Their meat was eaten, their oil was used for lamps and to waterproof fabrics, and the bones could be made into tools. The largest drive caught 1,540 whales at Quendale Bay in 1845. The last recorded drive, possibly shown here, was at Weisdale Voe in 1903 with a kill of 83 whales. Whaling become more industrialised in 1903/04 when four whaling stations were opened. These were the Zetland Whale Fishing Company and the Norrona Whale Fishing Company, both at Ronas Voe, the Alexandra Whaling Company at Collifirth, and the Olna Whaling Company at Voe, Olna Firth.

The Olna Whaling Company was owned by Christian Salvesen, based in Leith, and is featured above and overleaf. Whaling season was generally from April to September; Olna Firth station had four to five boats which could travel up to 150 miles into the whaling waters north of the islands. Whaling was suspended during the First World War; the Zetland and Norrona companies did not resume afterwards though Alexandra went on until 1921 and Olna closed in 1929. Overall, the stations caught nearly 7,000 whales, mostly Fin and Sei whales – the latter known to make a crying sound when killed – though this number includes over 80 Blue whales. Before the stations opened, Shetland men were involved in Greenland whaling; after their closure many went to South Atlantic and Antarctic waters to be employed on the whaling stations and factory ships Christian Salvesen operated there until the early 1960s. A Shetland man could return after 18 months with enough money to buy a house or a fishing boat of his own. During the First World War, the Royal Navy based a squadron of cruisers at Olna Firth and in 1915 it commissioned Da Voe Bakery to provide bread for the sailors; it is the oldest commercial bakery in Shetland.

Whales were caught with explosive harpoons and dragged back to stations by steamers. A steam winch brought them onto a slipway for processing. Here, the tongue of a whale is being removed and the men are preparing to flense it, separating the blubber from the muscle using long curved knives such as the one shown on the previous page. The carcass would then be stripped of its meat by lemmers (whale butchers). Whale oil was extracted by boiling the blubber and was used in the production of soap, margarine, lamp fuel and machine lubrication. British soldiers in the First World War rubbed it on their feet to prevent trench foot. Attempts to market whale meat for eating failed, so this was also boiled to produce oil, though of a lesser quality. Boilers could be 12 feet tall – a boiler house chimney can be seen. Whalebone was also used to produce thousands of products including baskets, corsets, umbrellas, back scratchers, shoe horns, cutlery, toys, carriage springs and tongue scrapers. Also called baleen, this material wasn't actually made from the bones of whales, but came from the bristles that were part of filter feeding systems inside some species' mouths – these are shown to the left of the whales carcasses in both photos. Jawbones were ground down to make whale meal for fertiliser.

Kelp is a common type of seaweed, though the name was once used for the soda ash that was created by burning it and used in the manufacture of soap, glass and paper. The production of 'kelp' was an important Scottish coastal industry between the late eighteenth century and the early 1900s. It was particularly important to Orkney and the Western Isles, but was carried out in Shetland too. A family endeavour for crofters, men collected the seaweed, children dragged it to dry it, and the women looked after the fires when the time came to burn it. Kelp burning took place between July and August, often using seaweed collected in the winter and spring months that had been dried on walls called kelp ricks (rainproofed with heather) and stored in buildings until needed. The seaweed was burned on metal grids laid over pits where the ash would collect. This was oily and would harden over a period of days or weeks into a blue solid mass. While still moderately soft, it would be divided by spades into more manageable blocks. Twenty tons of seaweed produced a single ton of kelp and it could be a hazardous business, the smoke and fumes being capable of causing blindness with prolonged exposure.

Horns of Soay sheep have been found at the prehistoric settlement of Jarlshof, so it is likely that sheep have been kept on Shetland for at least 4,000 years. Norse settlers brought their own sheep over and these ancient breeds contributed to the genetic makeup of current Shetland sheep, a small, hardy breed that has adapted to the harsh climate of the islands. The wool of this breed is fine yet strong, the fibres noted for their elasticity and loft. It has great insulation properties and is ideal for making garments that can be worn comfortably against skin. Due to cross-breeding with Norse sheep, Shetland fleeces grow in a range of colours from white to black with various shades of brown and grey in between, adding to its appeal. They can also produce wool suitable for both light and heavier weights of yarn. In 1580 the Scottish historian George Buchanan reported that Shetlanders made a living from selling 'a coarse thick cloth of a peculiar kind' to Norwegians. This was called 'wadmel' and hundreds of years earlier they had used this to pay tithes to the church and taxes to the ancient kings of Denmark.

Rooing Shetland Sheep. Photo J.D.Rattar.

By the 1600s Shetlanders were selling hand-spun stockings, gloves and night caps to English, German and Dutch traders. At this time, Shetland could only produce enough grain in a year to feed the population for three months and Orkney was supplying the shortfall in return for wool. In the 1870s there were over 90,000 sheep on Shetland and the wool industry was boosted from the 1920s by the growing popularity of Fair Isle-design knitwear. To stop the threat of cross-breeding from reducing stock quality, the Shetland Flock Book Society was established in 1927 to protect the breed. As the number of crofts fell throughout the twentieth century, more grazing land became available. Moorland was also converted to pasture through reseeding and fertilisation. Encouraged by EU subsidies, by the 1990s there were over 390,000 sheep in Shetland though the number has fallen by around 100,000 since. Nonetheless, the numbers remain huge, indicating the importance of sheep farming to the islands. Shetland sheep have also always been farmed for their meat, which is succulent and sweet, and for its qualities in meat and wool production they are bred in other parts of the world such as North America.

Shetland sheep shed their wool annually. This starts in late spring and there is a very obvious break or 'rise' between the new growth and the old which allows their wool to be simply plucked off rather than needing to be shorn. This process, known as 'rooing', is shown above and on the previous two pages. If done by practised hands, the fleece can come off in a single mass rather than in individual clumps. While they might feel the odd tug, the process should be painless to the sheep, though this seems to depend on who is doing the rooing – in his *Shetland: Descriptive and Historical* (1874), Robert Cowie described it as a 'barbarous process, giving much pain to the poor animals'. The wool is then bagged for the spinners. In Victorian times the sheep grazed freely on the 'scathold', or common ground, eating grass or seaweed at low tide, and ownership was denoted by different slits made in their ears. Before modern treatments were available, the sheep suffered from diseases such as braxy, foot rot, sturdy (coenurosis), and scab, the latter reducing some flocks by two-thirds in an outbreak in the 1770s. Due to their small size they could also be attacked by birds such as gulls, ravens, crows and eagles.

Besides coarser cloths, Shetland wool was used to knit lace, hosiery and delicate items such as ring shawls, so called because they could be pulled through a wedding ring. While fine knitting had been practised for hundreds of years, an industry in fine wool products grew from the 1830s, initially encouraged by the islands' MP, Frederick Dundas, who had been given a knitted 'invalid cap' by a Lerwick constituent. Impressed by its quality, he persuaded her and some others to make shawls; then, in 1839, an Oxford hosiery trader, Edward Standen, started selling the shawls into the London market. Meanwhile, Arthur Anderson, the Shetlander who co-founded the Peninsular and Oriental Steam Navigation Company (P&O), had given Queen Victoria some lace items as a coronation gift in 1838 and she subsequently ordered twelve pairs of lace stockings, starting a fashion for them. Soon patterns were being published in women's magazines and sewing manuals.

Carding and Spinning, Shetland. Photo – R. Williamson

Many young Shetland women started making lace items. By the 1870s the 'neat-fingered knitters of Zetland' were involved in an industry with a turnover of up to £12,000 per annum. Indeed, there was not enough Shetland wool to supply demand so some foreign wool such as Pyrenees wool and mohair was brought in. A collection of Shetland knitted clothing was presented to the Princess of Wales as a wedding gift in 1863, furthering its appeal. Spinning and carding the wool was evidently an activity that could be enjoyed outdoors on rare occasions when the weather was fine, though it's a wonder the cat isn't making off with some wool.

Before any items of clothing could be made the wool had to be combed or carded and then spun to produce wool yarn. Combing creates a denser fibre that can make a tighter and smoother worsted yarn, while carding creates fibres that make an airier yarn. The finest wool for creating lace yarn comes from round the neck of the sheep. Wool was washed to remove peat, dirt and vegetation, but some spinners preferred only light washing, if it all, and would comb/card and spin it with the natural oils of the sheep – the 'grease' – in because this enables the short fibres to stick together, allowing the fine gossamer threads required by lace to be spun. Shetland wool has a crimp which also helps the fibres to stay together. In this and the previous two photos the wool is being carded. This was the process of separating and straightening the wool, brushing it lightly back and forth between the carders, which had short teeth and are rather like large hairbrushes. Once all the fibres were separated out, the wool was removed from the carders and rolled into a rolag (derived from the Gaelic *roileag*). A number of rolags are gathered round the hearth in this 1930s photo.

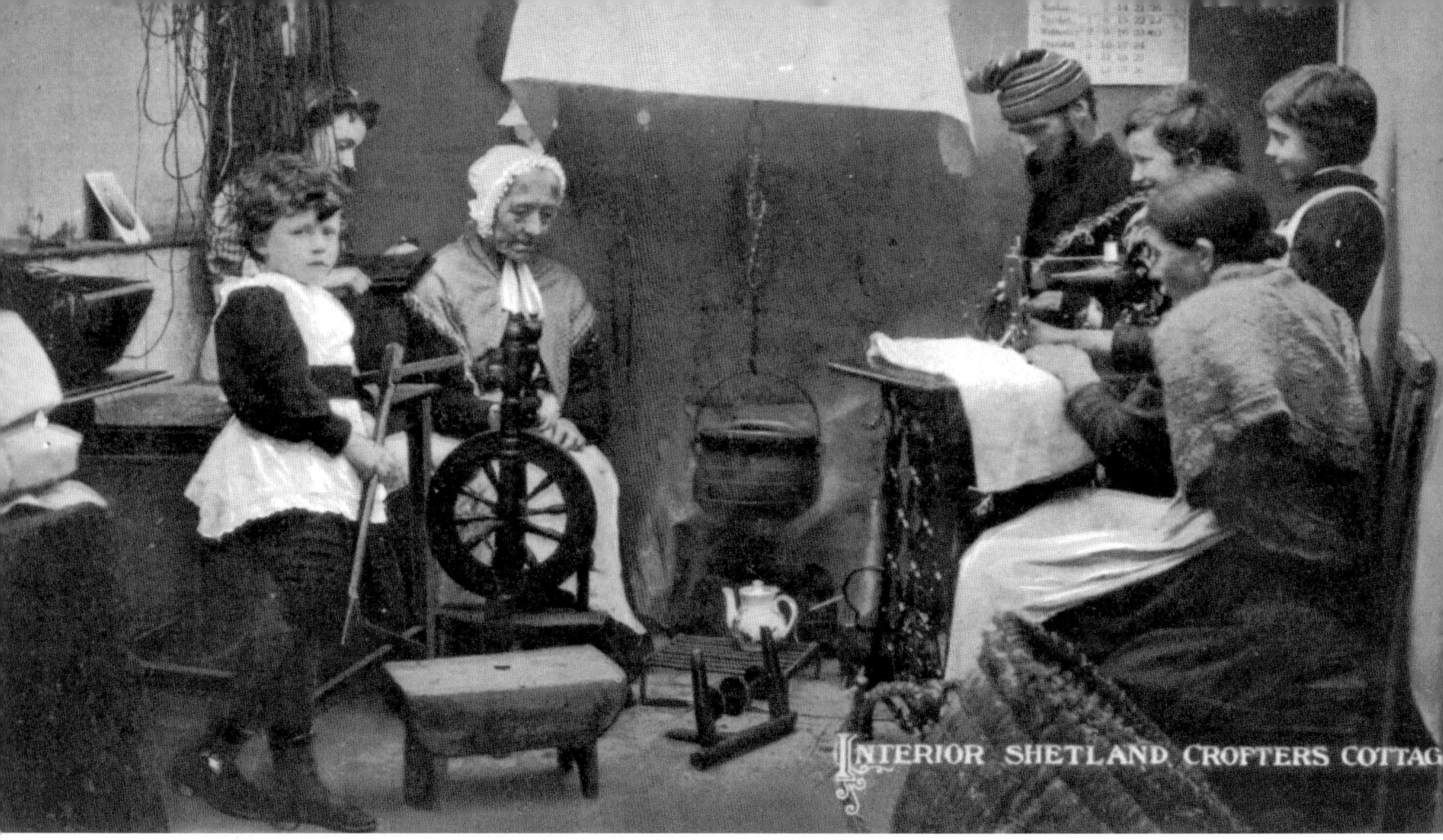

A Shetland spinnie was of a small, practical design and created the yarn. Carded wool was fed into the spinnie, powered by a foot pedal. The action of the spinnie twisted the wool into yarn which was collected onto a bobbin – one of these is on the floor in front of the teapot in this nineteenth century photo. There was much skill involved in spinning fine yarn and some women specialised only in spinning for lace. The women of Unst were particularly skilled lace spinners and knitters. By the 1860s lace was a high fashion item, decorating ladies' dresses not just on the Scottish mainland but from London to New York to Paris. Complex lace patterns could include cockle shell, fern, eyelid, Madeira diamond, with some patterns having names such as 'print o' waves' and 'old shale'. Purchasers tended to range from the upper classes to royalty. Not many Shetland women wore it themselves.

As with Fair Isle designs, the origins of lace patterns are essentially unknown, having been passed down from generation to generation. Many Shetland lace knitters used a knitting – or 'makkin'– belt. Worn at the waist, this was made from leather and had a pad stuffed with horsehair attached it, into which the end of a knitting needle could be put. This meant the knitter only needed to move the yarn with her right hand while the left did most of the movement; the wrists were hardly moved and the knitter would not be fatigued so quickly. The movements of the needles were also quicker, increasing the knitting speed, and the knitter could work while standing and even walking, with the ball of yarn attached to a hook at their waist. Shetland women spent much of their time knitting so the efficiency provided by the belt meant they could produce more items to increase their earnings. Some knitters were capable of doing 200 stitches a minute; some women even knitted as they carried creels of peat!

Once lace was knitted it was put in a smoking barrel to whiten it with sulphur smoke. Shawls then had to be 'dressed' to become the finished article. The shawl was washed and then stretched out and pinned within wooden frames as seen here. Wooden dowels were used to secure the shawls and the frames could be dismantled for easy storage. They were left to dry for 24 hours or more. This process was also known as 'blocking' and it opened out the pattern of the shawl so that it could be seen in all its glory. This photo may have been taken at the Lerwick premises of P.E. Petrie, described as a 'cleaner and dresser' of Shetland hosiery in a local trade directory.

This image shows the sheer size and intricacy of some shawls, giving an idea of the hours and labour involved in their creation.

It is unknown whether Norse settlers brought cattle but indigenous cattle certainly continued to be farmed by them, and butter and the 'ox penny' – per head of cattle – were paid as taxes. By the 1500s herds were growing and, as the human population increased, cattle became increasingly used for milk and beef, with their dung fertilising crops. Due to the lack of salt available to preserve meat, beef was air dried in small buildings known as 'skoes' and hides were used to make 'rivlins', a common form of footwear. By the early 1800s Shetland cattle numbered around 15,000, some of them being grazed on uninhabited islands. Oxen were prized for their strength as draught animals. While this 1911 photo shows a pair, four abreast were common with one man leading them and another working the plough. A household would usually not have more than one ox; others were borrowed from neighbours for ploughing.

The Shetland pony made a good substitute for the ox, though use of the latter was rare by the time of this 1950 photo, taken at Fladdabister. Agriculture has been essential to life on Shetland for at least 5,000 years. The earliest evidence of farming was found at Scord of Brouster on Mainland, where the remains of the farm site date back to 3400 BC. The climate was warmer then, with more trees on the islands, and this community lived among woodlands of birch, willow and hazel, which they cleared to create arable land fertilised with manure from their cattle and sheep, growing bere. Field systems developed and dykes were built to separate grazing land, which tended to be on the hill as more fertile soil was closer to the coast. Once Norse settlers arrived, townships of up to 20 houses were established, with the people working shared land and using barns, byres and kilns. On the southern part of Mainland, Fladdabister is notable for its limekilns, which were built in the nineteenth and early twentieth centuries to burn limestone and peat to produce quick lime for binding building stone. Much of this quick lime was sent to building works in Lerwick.

Opposite: After ploughing, the ground usually needed harrowed to break up clods of soil in order to create a seedbed, or to cover seed after it had been broadcast. The harrow was a horse-drawn frame with wooden or metal teeth. In the 1860s Robert Cowie noted that 'The harrow of this country differs only from that employed in Scotland by being of a smaller size, and having in most cases wooden teeth. In its locomotion – to the shame of the other sex be it said – the women are generally made beasts of burden. Sometimes, however, the pony does the work.' This 1905 postcard appears to have been staged by the woman in the picture, Kitty, as it carries a message to Jim: 'I thought perhaps you would like to have me leading a little beauty. Hope you will like it.' On the front of the card she wrote 'I must be smiling at you'! The dark mound behind Kitty is a potato 'clamp' – a heap of potatoes stored in an A-shaped row and covered with straw and soil to insulate them from the elements. Stored this way, they would remain edible for months.

For crofters, cultivating the land could be back-breaking work. In the 1800s, if a plough wasn't available, ground would often be broken up manually with spades. If there was no pony or ox, manure to fertilise crops was carried by women in creels. Springtime is called Voar in Shetland, and the time for sowing crops begins at the end of March. Oats were sown at the beginning of April and bere and potatoes at the beginning of May. In the autumn – or Hairst – hay was cut in August and bere and oats were ready for cutting in September. Reaping was done by sickle rather than scythe (though these could be used for mowing meadows) and the cut crops were assembled into stooks to allow them to dry. Crops could be destroyed by bad weather just before they were ripe. By the 1870s about 51,000 acres of Shetland were under cultivation, 11,600 under corn, but livestock numbers were climbing. At this time there were 22,000 cattle, 91,000 sheep, 6,000 horses and nearly 5,000 pigs.

After being cut and dried, corn was threshed with a flail to separate the heads from the stalks. Winnowing was required after this to separate the grain from the chaff created by threshing. By hand, this was done in breezy conditions whereby crofters would rub threshed corn between their hands, allowing the chaff to blow away and the heavier grains to fall onto a mat laid on the ground. The grains were then dried in a kiln and ground by a handmill in the crofter's barn, if he had one, or taken to a watermill. To the right of the man is a Shetland goose. Like other livestock on the islands, as befits the climate this breed is small and hardy and was kept by crofters to graze on pastures that would later be used for sheep, the geese preparing the ground by eating parasites such as liver fluke. The geese also provided meat, feathers and grease.

SHETLAND CORN MILL - EXTERIOR.

In the 1860s Robert Cowie described Shetland corn mills: 'The mill is a straw-thatched hut of the most primitive construction, and the smallest size calculated to admit human beings. The wheel is arranged so that the water is projected against it horizontally, and not perpendicularly, as in mills whose architects have rightly estimated the force of gravity.' Water was channelled down a stone-lined lade from a nearby burn and this pushed the paddle wheels which were positioned under the floor of the mill. These drove a fixed iron rod which turned the upper of the two millstones above. Having passed through the paddles of the upper mill, the water was directed back to the burn to power the mill downstream. Small mills such as these were family-owned or shared between up to three local families and were known as 'clack' mills due to the noise the paddles made as they worked. The location of the mills shown here is unknown but they are very similar to the surviving mills at Huxter in the west of Mainland. Those mills could grind a 22kg bushel of bere per hour, producing several sacks of flour. They stopped working in the 1940s but still stand, with one restored.

Horizontal mills were probably introduced by Norse settlers so their use may date back over a thousand years. They are mentioned in records dating from the fifteenth century and by the nineteenth century there were hundreds across the islands. While they didn't achieve the power of vertical water wheels, the horizontal design was easy to build and look after, using few materials and with no need of complicated gearing. *Left*: The paddle wheels – or tirls – were quite small, with around eight or nine small wooden blades fixed to a wooden centre (stone could also be used for this). *Above*: In the 'upper hoose' where the milling took place, a wooden hopper fed grain into the mill stones. The lower, thicker stone was fixed to the floor, while the thinner upper stone – fixed to the paddle wheel with a metal rod – rotated to grind the grain. Besides these small mills, there were three larger mills with conventional vertical wheels built in Shetland in the mid 1800s at Girlsta, Quendale and Weisdale.

Shetland ponies date back at least 2,000 years, with Bronze Age remains having been found at Jarlshof. Their exact origins are unknown but they possibly originated from Cob and Mountain ponies that migrated across the ice fields from southern Europe. Celtic ponies were brought over from the Scottish mainland around 1000 BC and Norse settlers brought their own small ponies too. The distinctive breed that subsequently evolved is small, strong and extremely hardy. Its height is usually between 28 and 42 inches and it has shorter legs than normal in relation to its size. It has large feet, ideal for marshy terrain, and a double-layered waterproof coat for protection from the elements. No matter the time of year, they are never stabled and live off grass and seaweed. Nonetheless, they can live in excess of 30 years. A common misconception is that Shetland conditions are responsible for their small size, but the climate has only bred hardiness into the animals. Those reared in fairer climes show no inclination of growing larger!

The ponies have always been used for work, pulling ploughs and carrying loads such as peat for burning and seaweed for fertilising in 'kishie' baskets woven from grasses. Even though they roam free, appearing to be wild, they were always marked by their owners who allowed them to graze freely on the scathold, bringing them in when needed for tasks. In the 1600s local fishermen made fishing lines from the hair of ponies' tails, which was also used to make the bows for fiddles. The Dutch fished for herring off Shetland from 1600 until 1892, between June and September each year, with the fleet sheltering off Lerwick. In the 1600s and 1700s riding the ponies was seen as a good way to exercise and they were hired out to Dutch sailors for this. The cliff known as 'Dutchman's Leap', at the Knab, south of Lerwick, supposedly got its name from a tragic incident when a sailor rode his pony a bit too enthusiastically and went over the edge.

Shipping Shetland Ponies

In 1842 the Coal Mines Regulation Act was passed by Parliament and from March the following year it was illegal for women and children to work in mines. This labour shortage was met by Shetland ponies, who were described by Robert Cowie as 'wonderfully hardy, sagacious and sure-footed' and could easily pull twice their own body weight – making them ideal for pulling loaded pit bogeys. They began to be sent south at a rate of around 1,000 a year and were also exported to America for mine work. Mine work was tough for the ponies and they spent most of their lives underground, usually only being brought to the surface for two weeks each year. They were essential workers though and treated well. The last recorded use of a Shetland pony in mine work was in America in 1971. Queen Victoria owned Shetlands and they were used to pull some of her carriages. They also became popular as a breed suitable for children to ride.

From the mid-nineteenth century breeding stock also began to be improved by studs that were established on the islands, at Tingwall, Noss and Bressay, the latter two set up in 1870 by the Marquis of Londonderry who needed ponies for his coal mines in England. Until 1899, when his stud was dispersed, he was greatly responsible for improving the stock, having selected six stallions of high quality for this purpose. This was a profitable business: males could fetch £10 and females up to £5. Prices of £30 for a very fine male were not unheard of. Due to the sudden worldwide popularity of the Shetland pony, fears grew about cross-breeding diminishing its quality and the Shetland Pony Stud Book Society was established in 1890 to preserve this. Jack of Noss – bred on Bressay – was the first pony in the book and most ponies today can be traced back to him. All Shetland ponies are logged and microchipped today.

Birds of Shetland, such as fulmars, puffins, auks and shags, were a crucial resource, hunted for food and other purposes. Birds were eaten fresh or preserved by salting, feathers were used for bedding and as fish bait, and oil was used in lamps. Indeed, the bird itself could become a lamp: twine was pulled through the carcasses of storm petrels to form a wick that would be kept alight by the oil in its flesh. Puffins and auks were caught in nets or were shot by those who owned guns. Burrow-nesting birds could also be caught on cliff faces, sometimes by hand and sometimes with a two-foot stick known as a 'croakie' on Foula and a 'kilpin' on Unst. Cliffs were divided between crofters and eggs were also gathered. It was a dangerous business dangling from a rope with a basket to collect the eggs. Sometimes the egg 'hunter' would work in bare feet to get better grip on the cliff face and he could also have a pole to help pull himself closer to nests. The ropes would either be held by others at the top of the cliff or tied to a stake. Boats were also used to reach remote cliff faces and the hunter would climb them from sea level. In the 1600s a pulley system was even devised at Noss so that eggs could be collected from the top of a rock stack. Unsurprisingly, fatalities are known to have occurred. If there was a large collection of eggs some were preserved by being dipped in isinglass, a substance similar to collagen which was obtained from fish bladders. Egg hunting died out in the early 1900s when there were greater food imports into the islands and also due to legislation which, largely due to the campaigning of the RSPB, began to be enacted to protect the bird population.

Peatland covers 12% of the land area of the United Kingdom. In Shetland the coverage is over 50% though this varies from area to area: it is very prevalent on Yell (where there were plans to build a peat-fired power station in the 1970s) though it is hardly present at all on Unst and Fetlar as the composition of the underlying rock prevents it from developing. Peat is created from decayed plantlife, mostly sphagnum moss, and the deposits have been built up over 4,000 years, reaching a depth of up to 20 feet in some areas. Ever since people settled in the Shetlands, it has been cut and dried and used as a fuel for heating and cooking. Even after burning it had a use, as peat ash made a very good fertiliser for kale and was also used to mark sheep. The processes of cutting, drying, transporting and storing peat were therefore integral to the life of Shetlanders for centuries. Crofters usually had peat-cutting rights on their land or used a communal bank, although some – such as those on Unst and Fetlar – had to travel far to get to their peat bank.

Cutting or 'casting' the peats took place in May. The first stage of this was to flay the moor with a tool called a ripper to remove the top layer of turf – or 'fael' – revealing the peat underneath. The exposed ground was then left to dry for a week or so and then casting could begin. This was the process of removing the peat from the ground with a tool called a 'tushkar', a long wooden handle with a narrow blade which had a right-angled part at the end of it (this can be seen in the photo above and the one on the facing page). The tushkar could easily cut through the soft peat. Cut peats were the size of the tushkar's feather, as the blade was called, usually a foot to fourteen inches long. Once pushed in, the peat cutter would turn the tushkar, the right-angled part at the bottom releasing the peat from the bank. The cutter would then place the cut peat at the top of the bank, creating a pile along the length of it as he worked.

Peat casting was methodical and rythmical, and men prided themselves on the neatness of their work. The outermost peat in each row was called a 'skyumpie'; smaller peats were called 'clods'. Cutting banks could be up to three metres deep and it was possible for a peat cutter – in Shetland they often worked alone – to cut enough peat in three days to last his family a year. Cut peats were laid along the bank in such a way as to allow air to flow between them so the drying process could begin as soon as they were cut. They were usually left like this for a week or so and then arranged into smaller pyramid-shaped piles of just a few peats for further drying. The women in this photo are engaged in this part of the process, which was called 'raising'. The small stacks could be rearranged over a few weeks to aid the drying process and then they were put back in larger piles, either for storage by the bank or for transportation.

This woman is working a length of knitting yarn as she carries her load. She has sensibly secured the peats so they won't fall out of her kishie as she walks. One can only hope she could look forward to a decent meal on her return home. To ensure there was enough to eat in winter months fish was dried and salted and there was 'reestit mutton'. For this a ewe was butchered and the meat was dried and salted. It was then left outside for further drying for three days or so and then soaked in a dense brine solution for around three weeks. The meat was then air-dried again for a day, usually being hung from a line, then it was hung above a peat fire for a month. When it came time to eat it, the meat had to be boiled and drained several times to make it soft and edible. Fish was preserved and later cooked in a similar way. The mutton was usually eaten with bannocks.

These women are efficiently doing their knitting as they carry their peats. The roads were rough but passable. The first road built in Shetland was the mile-long route from Lerwick to its nearest peat area, built in 1800. None followed until 1850, when it was decided they were needed to get supplies to remote families after a famine in 1848. These were built under military supervision and known as 'meal roads' as this was the form of payment to the labourers.

BRINGING HOME THE PEATS, UNST.   11133.

Shetland ponies were also used to transport the peats, these being strapped to their side either in kishies or in handmade rope panniers as seen in this photo from 1889, taken on Unst. Rope – 'simmens' – was made from rushes known as 'floss'. Wooden boxes were used too. Convoys of ponies driven by 'peat boys' were a common sight across the islands in mid summer. Unst didn't have much peat to begin with and on some parts of the island it had been all been worked out by the end of the eighteenth century. Crofters either had to use ponies to bring it over from existing peat banks at Valla Field or Saxa Vord or, having arranged a supply from Yell, transport it up from the south of the island. This was a laborious and expensive business and up to six weeks in the summer could be spent acquiring enough peats for the next twelve months.

Carts were also used if available – unlike this one! Again the women carrying the peats are knitting as they walk, the one on the left working on an item that seems to have reached quite an advanced stage.

Some peatlands were on higher ground, so ingenious methods such as this pulley system were devised to get the peats down. An 'endless' rope system was used so that the momentum of the loaded kishie going down would pull an empty one uphill where it would be refilled and returned. This photo, taken by Lerwick photographer John David Rattar, gives some idea of the steep heights peat could be worked at, though the location is not identified. It is known that a pulley system like this was worked at Levenwick in southern Mainland.

A crofter making a kishie while being warmed by peats burning in the fireplace. The lack of woodland on the islands, in particular willow, which was used for basket making in other parts of Britain, meant that soft rushes or marram grass and the rigid stems of oat straw and dock plants, or 'docken', were used instead. The latter made the body of the kishie while rushes or grass – dried to make them strong yet pliable – made the simmens that held the kishie together. Over 130 feet of simmens had to be created for a standard kishie and crofters would often get together in the evenings to make them in company. If docken was being used, the stems would need soaking for several hours so that they could be bent. To get the required rigidity into the kishie, three to four stems were gathered into a 'hjog' and this was bound together with the simmens. Kishies varied in size and purpose. Smaller ones tended to be made from docken and were used to gather bait and small fish while larger ones were of straw and used for larger items. New kishies were reserved for tasks like carrying groceries or items for sale; after they became more worn they were used for dirtier tasks like carrying peats and manure.

Finally, the peat would reach the croft. There it would be stored under cover, if outhouse space was available, or stacked with larger peats at the top to make a roof – dried peats form a water-repellent surface – to keep dry the smaller ones underneath. Crofters used peat to heat the home, cook the food and boil the water. The blackest peat was considered best as it would burn hotter and for longer due to its higher carbon content. A family could get through over ten thousand peats a year and peat later powered the Rayburn stoves that replaced the open fires in many homes. Its use declined as coal was sent to the islands and became more popular. It is much less used nowadays; indeed, the UK government plans to end the sale of bagged peat in 2024 and intends to phase out its use for other purposes over the next decade. Meanwhile, the peat banks are being restored in an initiative to return the peat bogs to their natural function as carbon sinks. Peatlands absorb carbon dioxide from the atmosphere through photosynthesis and, in effect, store it. UK peatlands 'lock in' around 3.2 billion tonnes of carbon.

A very tidy and productive example of a Shetland croft, positioned near the sea where the soil tended to be better, with crops on the arable areas and the pony on the upper scathold of the hillside. Most crofts had around three acres of land suitable for cultivation and another two of grass. The runrig system had been long been abandoned by the time J. D. Rattar took this photo and some crofts were already being amalgamated into larger concerns, especially to farm sheep. In terms of crops, in a particular growing area a crofter would usually grow potatoes in the first season, oats or bere in the second, followed by seasons for oats or bere, oats with grass seed, and then rye grass, with a fallow season to follow. Oats and potato crops were manured with compost created from turf, earth, seaweed and dung.

A typical croft near Scalloway, with a shed and byre attached. Often there would be a barn too. The byre was where cattle were kept and they were brought in every night. Robert Cowie noted that 'the bed of the cattle is formed by dry earth and turf from the scatholds. Whenever the floor becomes wet, a fresh layer of this material is laid over it without the previous one being removed. In this way the floor becomes more and more elevated, until the compost is obliged to be cleared away, in order to give the cattle head-room beneath the roof of the byre.' The barn was the place for storing food like potatoes and meal, which could also be ground in there with a hand mill. Most work was done by hand, even turning the field if there was no plough. Instead, crofters would 'dell' the ground, a process where up to three would work in a row with *cas chroms* – a digging tool with a narrow blade set on a pole with a peg so that the crofter could push it into the ground with the foot. Simultaneously, they would dig a trench while another member of the family, usually a child, would follow, sowing a crop such as seed potatoes from a bucket.

This croft was possibly near Hillswick, Mainland. The point of crofting was self-sufficiency for the crofter and his family, but this was often just at subsistence level and income had to be supplemented by fishing and knitting. Indeed, lairds forced many male tenants to fish for them as a means of paying their rents and they could be away for long periods in the fishing season of May to August, often remaining at fishing stations on their break days. The men would be at home for the seasons of peat cutting and harvesting, but otherwise the women were running the croft. When the herring industry became predominant this pattern remained the same, although this new fishing offered employment to women who came to the western ports to gut and pack herring in barrels. Once steam trawlers were introduced in the twentieth century, fishing became more of a full-time occupation for men and many left to join the whaling industry.

By the 1930s most crofts had up to four cows, ducks, geese, a pig and often around twenty sheep. Butter was made weekly and milk was also used to produce a soft cheese called 'kirn milk' and a drink called 'blaand'. Men would be 'away at da herrin'' while the women were at home keeping the croft going by feeding the livestock, milking, churning the milk, rooing sheep, looking after the crops, as well as raising the children. Other income came from knitting, which was done at every available minute, often in company in the evenings. The knitting industry was an important part of the local economy, though somewhat hidden as woollen items were often bartered for other goods so went unrecorded. From the end of the nineteenth century the more enterprising knitters used the cheap parcel post to sell items further afield.

Most croft houses had two rooms. The 'but end', seen here, was the main living space with seating and a fireplace; sometimes the latter would be in the middle of the floor. There were few windows and the interior was lit by lamps. Before the introduction of paraffin lamps, koli lamps were used. These were made from two iron pans, one suspended on top of the other. In the upper pan whale oil was burned with a wick, with the lower pan catching any overflowing oil. The upper pan was connected to the lower with a serrated bar so it could be adjusted to keep the oil level high enough to burn the wick. Kettles and cooking pots were suspended above the fire with a chain. The fire was always kept going, tamped down in the evening and brought back to life in the morning using bellows, were seen hanging above the fire. The 'ben end' was the bedroom, which was generally kept in neat order and used for receiving important visitors like the minister. The whole family slept in this room and box beds were used.

Another laborious task for the women was laundry, a job best done beside water where sheets and clothes could be beaten on rocks or with wooden bats, or trodden on within the large wooden basins.

A Shetland Darby & Joan.

Writing in his *Art Rambles in Shetland* (1869), John Reid paid tribute to the industry of the crofters and their wives: 'The male is in turn fisherman, farmer, mason, wright, weaver, tailor, tanner, shoemaker, boat builder; while his wife looks after the sowing and reaping, delving and weeding, the milking of the cow, churning, and the grinding of the corn or 'bere'. She plucks the wool off the sheep in a process called rooing, spins the yarn, and knits stockings that vary in price from fivepence to a guinea a pair, as well as a variety of other articles of Shetland hosiery. Moreover, she can row most skilfully, and has been known to display the courage of a Grace Darling by pulling out in the most tempestuous weather to the rescue of drowning fishermen.' He also noted that 'about one sixth of the householders are pretty well-to-do, about one half are from hand to mouth, and the remainder are in debt.' There is no question it was a tough life of endurance and back-breaking work though in the mid 1800s it was noted that generally Shetlanders had a better chance of making it to 70 than people in mainland Scotland. As Robert Cowie reported: 'I have frequently observed that Shetlanders retain the vigour and 'fresh' appearance of later manhood, or middle age, when far advanced in old age. Thus, I have seen a man of eighty-five row in a boat with two oars, with great agility and swiftness, amongst whose bushy locks incipient grey hairs could only be detected on close inspection, and who was supposed by an intelligent observer to be between fifty and sixty. Not unfrequently men upwards of eighty are found fully able for the extraordinary fatigue and exposure of the Shetland deep-sea fishing.'

Conditions for crofters steadily improved after the passing of the Crofters Holdings Act in 1886 which gave them land tenure rights and put a halt to the system of paying tithes to landowners. However, simultaneously, the industrialisation of the fishing industry offered new working opportunities to Shetlanders which meant that, increasingly, subsistence crofting was no longer necessary. Traditional crofting began to steadily disappear after 1945. As the twentieth century continued, more and more imported foods were brought to the island so it was no longer necessary for the population to grow its own supply. Tractors also started to appear on the islands – there were 29 by 1944 (mostly supplied by the Department of Agriculture) and jobs which usually took several people hours to do, such as cutting and turning hay, could now be carried out very quickly by one person. For many, crofting became a sideline or a hobby while they worked in the fishing and oil industries. From the 1970s there was a major switch to sheep farming as sheep are easy to keep and crofters could do other jobs and take care of their properties and flocks outside of working hours. In 1971 pasture land on Shetland was around 7,000 hectares; by 1999 this had risen to 20,000.